Faith Can Move Mountains

8 Essential Lessons on Faith

Faith Can Move Mountains

8 Essential Lessons on Faith

Dr. Derrick Justice

MASTER'S TABLE

ISBN 978-0-9994436-1-3

Contents

"Lord, I believe; help my unbelief!"

Other Books
by Derrick Justice

Derrick Justice
MINISTRIES

Prologue

With all that can be said about faith, the most important thing to point out is that the acquisition of or the failure to acquire it constitutes the determining factor as to your ultimate outcome in life. Faith is the key to what you do or don't do, and what you will accomplish or never attempt. If you want to do great things and experience God's best, then address your faith and the results will follow.

If you approach Jesus' earthly ministry with the intent on gleaning nuggets of wisdom for increasing your chances of being victorious in your everyday life, then you will quickly discover that the Lord spent a considerable amount of time addressing the apostles' faith. The Savior focused on their faith because he understood that they would have to build up a community that would face enormous opposition and challenges. Nevertheless, despite what would come against them, Jesus knew that if their faith was strong, then it would ensure their successful achievement against all odds and manner of opposition. With this book, you can learn the lessons the disciples learned that enabled them to prevail in any and every situation.

With this thoroughly researched and theologically sound eight-part study, you will be equipped with the understanding to usher in the kind of faith that will lead to victory for every area of your life. In addition, you will be able to teach transformative Bible studies as well as gain valuable tools to allow you to deliver powerful messages on faith.

Don't wait any longer. Get started today living in victory!

"Now Faith" Gives You "By Faith"

1

"NOW FAITH" GIVES YOU "BY FAITH"

¹Now faith is being sure of what we hope for and certain of what we do not see. ²This is what the ancients were commended for.
— *Hebrews 11:1–2*

Introduction

Faith has two components: 1) The first component is **surety**, "faith is being sure of what we hope for," and 2) the second component is **certainty**, "and certain of what we do not see" (Hebrews 11:1). "Now faith is being sure of what we hope for and certain of what we do not see."

The writer then says, "This is what the ancients were commended for." The "ancients," or more appropriately the heroes of the faith, were appreciated and praised because they had surety and certainty despite what they were facing.

Faith that God applauds has to be sure, and it has to be certain. What you have the capacity to hope for is up to you, but if you want God to commend it, then what you hope for must be grounded and anchored in surety and certainty.

If you are sure and if you are certain, then you have what the Bible calls "now faith," and "now faith" leads to your "by faith." That is, you will get the healing *by faith*. You will get the promotion *by faith*. You will reclaim what you were meant to have *by faith*.

Discussion

Real faith produces results. You will never get "by faith" without having "now faith," but if you have now faith, then you will definitely get some by faith results.

These two components of faith are found in the lives of every story of great faith.

• Abraham was enabled to bear a son even when he was past the age because he was sure and he was certain of it.

• Abel offered up a better sacrifice than his brother Cain because he was sure and he was certain of it.

• Moses made it through the Red Sea (i.e., the Sea of Reeds) because he was sure and he was certain that he would come out on the other side.

• When the walls of Jericho were crumbling down, Rahab, the hooker who protected the Israelite spies, made it out of the devastation because she was sure and she was certain God would repay her faithfulness (Joshua 2:1–14; Matthew 1:5–6; Hebrews 11:31).

You can have faith, but if it's not sure and certain faith, then it's not the kind of faith that pleases God.

What God looks for when you're facing opposition, or when you're in a trying situation that is causing you to struggle in your belief, is whether you're *sure* and *certain* He's going to honor and reward your faith.

But if you lose your confidence in God, then you'll lose your reward from God (Hebrews 10:35–36). You must know for certain that God will absolutely reward your confidence in Him.

However, here is the plain truth: When you have "now faith," you're going to have some now problems— i.e., real faith is met with real trials and tribulations, and bad experiences and suffering are designed to steal your confidence in God.

In this light, Paul says, "We are hard pressed on every side, but not crushed; perplexed, but not in despair; persecuted, but not abandoned; struck down, but not destroyed" (2 Corinthians 4:8–9). Walking by faith is difficult and met with every attack and hardship the enemy can throw at you, but regardless of what may come your way, you will prevail *by faith.*

When God shines His light in your life, you then have the treasure of faith in your heart, and you just know that God is: God is real. God has all power in His hand. God can do all things but fail. Yes, God is.

When you know that God is, it's like light that shines into the darkness. In the beginning, God created the heavens and the earth. The earth was without form and void, and darkness was on the face of the deep. Then God said, "Let there be light, and there was light" (Genesis 1:1–3). The light says God is.

Once light shines into darkness, darkness has no more power over the light. Thus, you know that darkness has no more power over you.

The pain and stress that is associated with darkness may come into your life for a short while, but faith says the light of morning is on the way (Psalm 30:5).

Conclusion

Faith is like the morning. No matter how dark the night gets, morning is on the way. As long as you know the morning is going to come, you can make it through the roughest of nights. Faith helps you make it through the dark and the difficult times in your life.

When you have **now faith**, it says your **by faith** is coming. It's in the mail; it's on the direct flight; it's being expressed delivered. It's coming!

You might not know how long the struggle is going to last, but I can tell you that your "by faith" testimony is on the way.

Faith & Action
Lesson One

1) *What did you learn about your faith from this chapter? (Be specific)*

_____

_____

_____

_____

_____

2) *In what area(s) of your life can you apply what you learned?*

_____

_____

_____

_____

_____

3) *"Prayer changes things." Pray first, then take action in an area(s) of your life according to your faith.*

Action Area 1:

Action Area 2:

Faith Journal

_____

_____

_____

_____

_____

_____

_____

_____

_____

_____

_____

_____

_____

_____

_____

_____

_____

FAITH CAN MOVE MOUNTAINS
Testimony Journal

_____

_____

_____

_____

_____

_____

_____

_____

_____

_____

_____

_____

_____

_____

_____

_____

_____

Turn Your Faith Into Power

2

TURN YOUR FAITH INTO POWER

Then the devil left him, and angels came and attended him.
—Matthew 4:11

Introduction

A man came to Jesus, knelt before him, and asked the Lord to have mercy on his son. His son was demon possessed, and the demon would cause the boy to have seizures; the satanic agent would at times even throw the child into the fire or water in an attempt to kill him. The man wanted Jesus to heal his son. Jesus did, but after the service was over, Jesus' disciples wanted to know why they couldn't drive the demon out themselves. Jesus explained to them, "[If] you have faith as small as a mustard seed, you can say to this mountain, 'Move from here to there, and it will move. Nothing will be impossible for you'" (Matthew 17:20).

What you are looking at in Jesus' answer and in his performance is faith that has been turned into power. Faith can be passive or active. Powerful faith is not passive faith that's waiting to be healed of some infirmity. This is faith that takes action against obstacles and strongholds. Powerful faith is operative and assertive.

You can have faith but not power, or you can have faith that operates in power. The choice is yours.

Discussion

How to turn your faith into power.

Anyone who says he's a part of the community of faith is what we who lead in the Church call a baptized believer. Baptism is how one enters into the Christian community. Baptism is an outward sign of an inward confession (Mark 16:16; Romans 6:3–4).

When Jesus went before John the Baptist to be baptized, John immediately recognized who the Lord was, and he said to Jesus, "I need to be baptized by you," indicating that Jesus was sinless, but Jesus replied, "Let it be so now; it is proper for us to do this to fulfill all righteousness" (Matthew 3:15). Jesus' baptism was an example to anyone who would follow him. Everyone needs to be baptized.

But immediately after baptism, the Holy Spirit led Jesus into the wilderness to be tempted by the devil. After

forty days of fasting—i.e., Jesus was at his weakest—
then the test commenced.

1) The devil said, If you are the Son of God, tell these
stones to become bread. Jesus replied, "It is written:
'Man does not live on bread alone, but on every word
that comes from the mouth of God'" (Matthew 4:4).

   POINT: The devil will always test the weakness of
your flesh. Will the desires of your flesh dictate what you
do, or will the word of God determine what you do? Put
another way, do you go by what you feel or by what
God's word says? Determining in your heart to follow
God's holy word is one of the hardest things you will
ever deal with as a person. You have two (2) responses to
God's word. One, rejecting God's instructions will bring
you down (Psalm 50:17–21); two, following God's
instructions will lift you up (1 Samuel 15:22).

2) The devil took Jesus to the holy city (i.e., Jerusalem),
and he told him, "[Throw] yourself down. For it is
written: 'He will command his angels concerning you,
and they will lift you up in their hands, so that you will
not strike your foot against a stone,'" but Jesus replied,
"It is also written: 'Do not put the Lord your God to the
test'" (Matthew 4:7).

   POINT: The devil will try to get you to test the
faithfulness of God. In other words, he will prompt you

to go do this or that to prove God's faithfulness. This is a sin because it is a challenge to God to do what it is you want according to when you want it and not according to when God ordains it, which is to say, **God, prove to me now that you are who you say you are**." However, real faith says God doesn't have to prove Himself to you because you trust in Him regardless of whether He does what you want or what He knows is best, and trusting in Him establishes the truth of your faith which God will ultimately reward.

3) Finally, the devil showed Jesus all the kingdoms of the world and their splendor, and he told Jesus, *If you bow down and worship me, I'll give you all this*, but Jesus told him, "Worship the Lord your God, and serve him only" (Matthew 4:10).

    POINT: The devil was saying if you don't resist me, I'll give you everything your heart desires. Just do it my way, and you'll get it all. To put it more directly, don't do it God's way. However, it's either your way or God's way. Resisting the devil is hard. It's not easy to fight the good fight of faith. Yet, faithful people resist the devil, and unfaithful people give in to the temptation.

    RESULT: Jesus resisted the devil, and the Bible says the devil left him. **Key**: After the devil left him, angels came and ministered to him (v. 11). This angelic response to having gone through such a grueling spiritual test is where Jesus' faith got the power so that it could work for the benefit of others. But he first had to resist until his enemy left him. As a result, every time he shows up, the enemy is reduced to having to surrender and back down in defeat.

Follow Jesus' example, and you will get the same result. The enemy can look at you coming and say, *Here comes a chump in the faith,* or he can look at you and say, *I am already defeated because that one there is not playing around with the faith but taking it seriously. That one is operating in power.*

By knowing the word of God and resisting the devil, you will turn your faith into putting-the-enemy-on-the-run power.

Conclusion

James 4:7 confirms, "Submit yourselves, then, to God. Resist the devil and he will flee from you."

Baptism is what? An outward sign of an inward confession. Resisting the devil is when you start living according to what you say you believe despite how tough the tests in life may be. When you do, you're washing your spirit (John 13:10), and God in response gives your faith real world-changing, yoke-removing, burden-destroying, tongue-talking power!

Faith & Action
Lesson Two

1) What did you learn about your faith from this chapter? (Be specific)

_____

_____

_____

_____

_____

2) In what area(s) of your life can you apply what you learned?

_____

_____

_____

_____

_____

3) "Prayer changes things." Pray first, then take action in an area(s) of your life according to your faith.

Action Area 1:

Action Area 2:

Faith Journal

Testimony Journal

_____

_____

_____

_____

_____

_____

_____

_____

_____

_____

_____

_____

_____

_____

_____

_____

Great Faith

3

GREAT FAITH

⁵When Jesus had entered Capernaum, a centurion came to him, asking for help. ⁶"Lord," he said, "my servant lies at home paralyzed and in terrible suffering."
⁷Jesus said to him, "I will go and heal him?"
⁸The centurion replied, "Lord, I do not deserve to have you come under my roof. But just say the word, and my servant will be healed. ⁹For I myself am a man under authority, with soldiers under me. I tell this one, 'Go,' and he goes; and that one, 'Come,' and he comes. I say to my servant, 'Do this,' and he does it."
¹⁰When Jesus heard this, he was astonished and said to those following him, "I tell you the truth, I have not found anyone in Israel with such great faith. ¹¹I say to you that many will come from the east and the west, and will take their places at the feast with Abraham, Isaac and Jacob in the kingdom of heaven. ¹²But the subjects of the kingdom will be thrown outside, into the darkness, where there will be weeping and gnashing of teeth."
¹³Then Jesus said to the centurion, "Go! Let it be done just as you believed it would." And his servant was healed at that very hour.
—Matthew 8:5–13

Introduction

The Story of the Centurion makes one point perfectly clear: Anyone can have great faith. When a person with great faith asks the Lord for help, the Prince of glory will not hold it against the person that he is not a great person, but He will instead reward him because he is a person of great faith.

Discussion

There are three (3) ways to look at faith:
a) Lack of faith
b) Faith
c) Great faith

One: A lack of faith says there is simply no faith, or very "little faith," with which Jesus can work.

Note that it is not that the Lord's ability to heal, bless, etc. is dependent upon our faith. Rather, he chooses not to act because of the lack of our faith.

For example, the people in Jesus' hometown took offense at him because they couldn't figure out where he got such wisdom and ability (Mark 6:1–6).

In response, Jesus said, "Only in his hometown, among his relatives and in his own house is a prophet without honor." Because of their lack of faith, Jesus could only lay hands on a few sick people and heal them.

He was amazed at their lack of faith, so he went to another village.

Two: Faith in the Lord is powerful and gets results.
a) The woman with the issue of blood had faith, and Jesus said her faith healed her (Mark 5:25–34).
b) Two blind men had faith, and Jesus told them according to your faith it will be done unto you, and their sight was restored (Mark 20:29–34).
c) A man by the name of Bartimaeus used to sit by the road and beg. One day he heard Jesus was passing by, and he started shouting, "Jesus, Son of David, have mercy on me!" People tried to rebuke him and tell him to shut up, but that made Bartimaeus shout even more. Jesus heard him and called him. The Lord asked him, "What do yo want me to do for you?" Bartimaeus said, 'Rabbi, I want to see.' Jesus said, "Go . . . your faith has healed you" (Mark 10:46–52).

Interestingly, Jesus knew Bartimaeus was blind and must have wanted his sight, but it is the opinion of this author that Jesus simply wanted him to request it in faith. Is he waiting for you to speak in faith as to what it is you truly want him to do for you?

Three: Great faith is what the Centurion had.
There are only two (2) occasions in the entire Bible in which Jesus assessed someone's faith and

declared that the person had "great faith": a) the centurion and b) a Canaanite woman with a demon-possessed daughter.

What is similar about the centurion and the Canaanite woman is that neither was a Jew. Neither of them had a cultural or religious basis with which to believe in Jesus. They both came to him because they both had a bad problem, and they had heard he could fix whatever problem(s) a person has.

There are three (3) things to know about Great Faith:
1)   The centurion didn't go to Jesus because he needed the Lord personally. He went to Jesus because someone else needed him.

Great faith is not selfish. Sometimes other people need for you to go to the Lord on their behalf.

2)   The centurion did not feel worthy to be granted a miracle.

When Jesus responded to the centurion's request for healing for his servant, he said, "I will go and heal him," but the centurion said, "Lord, I do not deserve to have you come under my roof."

Notice that the centurion called Jesus "Lord." He was not a believer in Jesus in terms of being a disciple, but he was humble in the presence of the Lord.

Great faith is humble faith. Humility puts the
authority of Jesus over all things. If you want a miracle in
your life from the Lord, humble yourself before him.
Don't be too proud or sophisticated to humble yourself in
the presence of the Lord Almighty. Your breakthrough
may just hang in the balance.

3)   Great faith does not have a spirit of entitlement
before God, but it appeals to the mercy of God.
        Jesus asserted that "many will come from the east
and the west, and take their places at the feast of
Abraham, Isaac and Jacob in the kingdom of heaven. But
[they] will be thrown outside . . . where there will be
weeping and gnashing of teeth." A spirit of entitlement
gets rebuked; appealing to the Lord's mercy gets a
miracle.

Conclusion

        Great faith says you might have some flaws, but
you approach the Lord asking God for mercy, not
because you think you are entitled to a miracle. Great
faith expects God to move because of who He is and not
because of who you are.
        Great faith says you'll pray just as hard for
someone else as you will for yourself.
        Finally, great faith steps out in belief. It doesn't sit
around, tapping its fingers on the table, waiting for the

Lord to pass by or just happen to be in the neighborhood; oh no, great faith goes and finds where the Lord is working, and then it humbly becomes a part of what God is doing.

Faith & Action
Lesson Three

1) *What did you learn about your faith from this chapter?*
(Be specific)

_____

_____

_____

_____

_____

2) *In what area(s) of your life can you apply what you*
learned?

_____

_____

_____

_____

3) *"Prayer changes things." Pray first, then take action in*
an area(s) of your life according to your faith.

Action Area 1:

Action Area 2:

Faith Journal

_____

_____

_____

_____

_____

_____

_____

_____

_____

_____

_____

_____

_____

_____

_____

_____

Testimony Journal

_____

_____

_____

_____

_____

_____

_____

_____

_____

_____

_____

_____

_____

_____

_____

_____

_____

_____

_____

Wait on the Lord

4

WAIT ON THE LORD

[1]I will stand at my watch
and station myself on the ramparts;
I will look to see what he will say to me,
and what answer I am to give to this complaint.
[2]Then the Lord replied:
"Write down the revelation
and make it plain on tablets
so that a herald may run with it.
[3]For the revelation awaits an appointed time;
it speaks of the end
and will not prove false.
Though it linger, wait for it;
it will certainly come
and will not delay.
[4]"See, he is puffed up;
his desires are not upright—
but the righteous person will live by his faith
—Habakkuk 2:1–4

Introduction

Faith has wonderful benefits—you can get healed by faith, you can cast out demons by faith, you can get back what you lost by faith, you can overcome tremendous obstacles and setbacks by faith, and your faith can effect a blessing in other people's lives; however, faith has one issue that most people do find troubling, and thus it makes the prospect of faith perplexing: **Faith means waiting, and waiting is not always easy**.

God doesn't always do what you believe Him to do the minute you want it. God will do it in His time, and sometimes He will simply say wait. God will leave you in trying and difficult situations, and while you're dealing with your painful circumstances, He'll say just believe. Thus, while you're waiting, you got to keep exercising your faith.

Discussion

But the prophet Habakkuk had the audacity to get so frustrated about having to wait that he said God was going to have to tell him why. Eventually, God did answer and explain why, and one writer says this exchange between the prophet and the Lord gives today's believers one of the most important and indisputable theophanies[1] in the Bible.

In other words, if you want to understand why the Lord will make you wait for your miracle, then it is right here that you will find out why. This event between God and Habakkuk is actually the key to the point of the entire Bible.

Habakkuk was frustrated for having to wait so long for God to move. He was a man of great faith, but because he had to wait so long, he started having doubts. He waited so long that he became troubled down in his soul, and after a while, he started complaining.

It got so bad that Habakkuk said he was just going to stay on the ramparts, i.e., a wall-like ridge, until the Lord answered him, and when He did answer, Habakkuk knew exactly what he was going to say in response.

Eventually, God told the frustrated prophet to write the revelation down and make it plain, and anyone who reads it can take it and run with it because it was sure to happen.

God told Habakkuk it might take a while, but "though it linger," it will certainly come (v. 3).

Then God gave the statement that scholars and people of great faith have come to realize is the central message of the entire Bible. If you want to know what the word of God is all about, it's right here.

---

[1] A theophany is a visible manifestation of God.

God told Habakkuk when I tell people to wait, the proud person will get puffed up, and that tells Me his soul isn't right, but the just shall live by faith (v. 4). Waiting may hurt, but waiting makes your faith strong, and it reveals who you truly are.

Waiting tells God whether you're just or whether you're puffed up.

A puffed up person will get mad and tired, and tell God, *I'll do it myself,* but when just people have to wait, waiting makes them worship. Waiting enriches your soul and your faith, and the result is pure praise and worship.

For instance, Aaron the priest had four sons, and they were next in line to be the priests for the people when Aaron's time was up. But while they were waiting, they were to help their father.

But the two oldest sons, Nadab and Abihu, got tired of waiting, so they took their sensors and offered up fire in them, but God said this was strange fire, and no one was to offer up strange fire before the Lord, and the fire they offered up turned around and consumed them (Leviticus 10:1–7).

By contrast, the two other sons who waited, they were called by Moses to receive the blessing associated with being priests. Because they waiting on God, they got blessed by God.

When you wait, you'll get the blessing. Waiting is tough, but the Lord told Habakkuk, it is certain to happen. Though it may linger, wait on it.

The principle of waiting and blessing comes from the father of the faith, Abraham. Abraham was old, but he waited on the Lord, and because he believed the Lord, the Bible says, "[The Lord] credited it to him as righteousness" (Genesis 15:6).

Now if you're a business-minded person, you know that in business there are debits and there are credits.

In a business account, debits reflect all of the money flowing into the account, while credits record all of the money flowing out of the account.

When you do business with God, you have what I like to think of as a faith account. When you believe God, that's a debit into your account; when you doubt God, that's a credit of your account.

Abraham believed God, and God took from His account (which was a credit on His account but a debit to Abraham's) and deposited it into Abraham's account—a debit.

Conclusion

When you live by faith, the Lord just keeps crediting righteousness to your faith account, and as it says in the book of Hebrews, one day you will have a harvest of righteousness (Hebrews 12:11).

Your faith justifies your harvest.

David says, "Wait on the Lord; be strong and take heart and wait for the Lord" (Psalm 27:14).

Your harvest will make the wait worth it.

Faith & Action
Lesson Four

1) *What did you learn about your faith from this chapter? (Be specific)*

_____

_____

_____

_____

_____

2) *In what area(s) of your life can you apply what you learned?*

_____

_____

_____

_____

3) *"Prayer changes things." Pray first, then take action in an area(s) of your life according to your faith.*

Action Area 1:

Action Area 2:

Faith Journal

_____

_____

_____

_____

_____

_____

_____

_____

_____

_____

_____

_____

_____

_____

_____

_____

Testimony Journal

The Man Born Blind

5

THE MAN BORN BLIND

[1]As he went along, he saw a man blind from birth. [2]His disciples asked him, "Rabbi, who sinned, this man or his parents, that he was born blind?"
[3]"Neither this man nor his parents sinned," said Jesus, "but this happened so that the work of God might be displayed in his life. [4]As long as it is day, we must do the work of him who sent me. Night is coming, when no one can work. [5]While I am in the world, I am the light of the world."

—John 9:1–5

He replied, "Whether he is a sinner or not, I don't know. One thing I do know. I was blind but now I see!"

—John 9:25

Introduction

One of the things I have always wondered about is why God will wait so long (it seems) before He decides to bless certain people. Some people seem to be born blessed and with all the advantages. Others are born, as it often seems, with all kinds of disadvantages.

Discussion

Take, for instance, the man born blind. Yes, he was born blind. He never had sight. He was never born with the chance to be successful. He was never allowed to do what the other people could do. He was born in a disadvantaged predicament.

He was born needing help and needing assistance. When other people could go out and make decisions for themselves and have the opportunity to determine their course in life, all this man could do from the time he came into the world was sit and beg and hope that others would show him mercy.

His situation in life was so pathetic that it prompted Jesus' disciples to look for the reason of his condition. "Rabbi, who sinned, this man or his parents, that he was born blind?"

The implications of the question are tremendous. Either God was punishing the man for sins he had yet to commit, or God was punishing him because of his parents' sins.

But Jesus' answer is just as shocking: "Neither this man nor his parents sinned . . . but this happened so that the work of God might be displayed in his life" (v. 3).

God let everything go wrong in the man's formation so that the work of God could be displayed in his life.

Put another way, there are some people selected for the sole purpose of being a display and the evidence of what God can do. But in order for the display/evidence to be convincing, the condition has to be so bad that when God does fix it, there can be no doubt that it was anyone other than the Lord who did it.

The man was selected to be God's display of what Jesus can do when he shows up in someone's life.

It wasn't the mud that Jesus put on the man's eyes that did it (John 19:6). It was faith in Jesus that did it. It wasn't the pool of Siloam that the man washed in that did it (John 19:7). It was faith in Jesus that did it.

The Account

1) The Pharisees asked the man how he had received his sight. The man told them, "He put mud on my eyes, and I washed, and now I see" (John 9:15). The Pharisees, however, argued that Jesus did it on the Sabbath.

2) Then the Pharisees wanted to know what the man had to say about Jesus (after all, it was his eyes Jesus opened). The man then told them, "[Jesus] is a prophet" (John 9:17). The Pharisees then chose to believe that the man wasn't really born blind.

3) When the Jews didn't get the answer for which they were looking, they then sent for the man's parents, and the interrogators wanted to know, "Is this your

son? Is this the one who had been born blind? How is it that now he can see?" The parents said, yes, this is our son. Yes, he was born blind. But how he got his sight, this we can't tell you. You will have to ask him. (John 9:18–21).

4) The Pharisees called the man back to witness a second time. They told him, "Give glory to God," which is another way of saying now tell the truth because "We know [Jesus] is a sinner." The man who had been born blind replied, "Whether he is a sinner or not, I don't know. One thing I do know, I was blind but now I see."

The man came into the world without vision, but the man they call Jesus gave him his sight.

There was nothing wrong with the man's mind. There was nothing wrong with the man's legs, and neither was there anything wrong with his arms. All of which is to say, you can have a lot of problems in life, but when you don't have vision, you can't be who you have the potential to be; you cannot try things other people can try. On the other hand, when you have vision, your world changes. The psalmist writes where there is no vision, people will perish (Proverbs 29:18). However, where there is vision, people will prosper.

You must have vision if you're going to succeed, and the Lord will give you vision. Jesus gave the man his eyesight, and the man's life changed. He became a display of the goodness of God.

When they called him in to testify, the man who had been born blind said, "One thing I do know, I was blind but now I see" (John 9:25). There has never been a more faithful statement. The man born without sight became one amazing piece of evidence of what the power of God can do in a person's life. Through faith, God can restore everything and anything you are meant to have.

Conclusion

Some people are meant to be a display of what God can do. Some people are called to witness for God not because of their brains, not because of their talent, but because of the problem(s) they had and how the power of God turned their problems in to their testimonies.

There is no greater honor than to be called to be the evidence of how faith in the Lord can turn a problem into a powerful testimony.

Faith & Action

Lesson Five

1) What did you learn about your faith from this chapter? (Be specific)

_____

_____

_____

_____

_____

2) In what area(s) of your life can you apply what you learned?

_____

_____

_____

_____

_____

3) "Prayer changes things." Pray first, then take action in an area(s) of your life according to your faith.

Action Area 1:

Action Area 2:

Faith Journal

_____

_____

_____

_____

_____

_____

_____

_____

_____

_____

_____

_____

_____

_____

_____

_____

_____

_____

Testimony Journal

_____

_____

_____

_____

_____

_____

_____

_____

_____

_____

_____

_____

_____

_____

_____

_____

Faith and Racism

6

FAITH AND RACISM

⁷When a Samaritan woman came to draw water, Jesus said to her, "Will you give me a drink?" ⁸(His disciples had gone into the town to buy food.)
⁹The Samaritan woman said to him, "You are a Jew and I am a Samaritan woman. How can you ask me for a drink?" (For Jews do not associate with Samaritans.)
¹⁰Jesus answered her, "If you knew the gift of God and who it is that asks you for a drink, you would have asked him and he would have given you living water."
—John 4:7–10

Introduction

Every person of color has a personal account of some form of racism. In fact, everyone—minority and majority—has some personal experience with racism.

The history of racism in America and around the world goes all the way back to the beginning of time. Everyone has been impacted by it in some way.

It will surprise most people that even Jesus had his own encounter with the ugly reality of bigotry and discrimination.

Discussion

Background
• Jews were full-blooded, and they were also monotheistic, meaning they worshipped only one God.
• Samaritans (2 Kings 17:24) were mixed and considered corrupt and ritually impure. They were polytheistic (2 Kings 17:29–41; Ezra 9:1–10, 44; Nehemiah 13: 23–28), meaning they worshipped many gods.
• There was a wall of bitterness between the two groups (Ezra 4). They were completely divided by racial and ethnic barriers. Note that lies about people who are different maintain barriers, which is still true today.

• Jews didn't associate with Samaritans, and Samaritans didn't speak to Jews.
• For Jesus to talk openly with a Samaritan woman was absolutely shocking.
• Jews and Samaritans were segregated; they worshipped in different temples. Jews, for instance, worshipped in the Jerusalem temple, and Samaritans worshipped on Mount Gerizim.
• Racism makes it more difficult to love and relate to people we see everyday than people who, for example, live on the other side of the world; racism says people whose skin color, language, values, history, and customs are different can't be trusted or appreciated.

Jesus was at the well when the woman arrived around noonday to draw water. They didn't salute or greet one another. There were no pleasantries, only avoidance and indifference. They were just two people who happened to be at the same place at the same time.

Jesus was exhausted and thirsty, and the Samaritan woman had what he needed because she had a water jar with which to draw water, but Jesus, in turn, also had what she desired (i.e., an opportunity for a different way of life) although she didn't realize it. All she saw was Jesus' race and his culture, so she thought she knew about him and what he thought of her.

The Woman as the Perpetrator of Racism: The foreign woman was a mixed-race person. It was said of Samaritan women that they were "menstruants" from the cradle, which stereotypically said in the colloquialism of the day that they were born sexually active. However, she seemed to live up to the racist stereotype because she had been married and divorced five times. Furthermore, she was living with a man to whom she was not married. In the eyes of a typical Jew, she was an immoral woman.

The Bible says that Samaritans "followed worthless idols and themselves became worthless" (2 Kings 17:15). The typical Jew would see a woman like her as worthless, but of course Jesus is not typical. He does not think of anyone in a certain way just because others want to think of them in a particular hurtful way.

When Jesus asked the woman for a drink of water, she responded to the perception she had of his race and not his character. She only saw him as a Jew and what she thought he thought of her. She didn't see the opportunity of the meeting—only the pain associated with her past.

Being racist didn't mean she was a bad person. She was an honest person. When Jesus told her to go back and get her husband, she replied, "I have no husband."

Her honesty said she was the type of worshipper God was looking for. Jesus later explained that the Father seeks people who worship in spirit and truth (John 4:24).

Jesus as the Victim of Racism: Jesus didn't let the woman's view of him stop him from being what he is about: turning people's lives around. When he asked her to give him a drink of water and she judged him, he did not let that affect him or alter his character.

Jesus was no stranger to being racially insulted; the Jews once called him a "Samaritan," which was a major insult (John 8:48). Despite what she errantly thought about him, he knew she could benefit from knowing who he truly was even though she had not yet realized it.

When she finally admitted she wanted the water that only he could give her—i.e., living water, he then told her to go home and bring her husband back. But she didn't understand he was actually testing her character. The woman had faith, but she was also a racist; however, what she was on the outside masked who she was on the inside. She was actually an honest person.

Jesus discovered her prejudice toward him was handed down to her—she had been taught and conditioned to be who she was. Nevertheless, she indeed had faith, but she worshipped what she did not know (v. 22). Her faith and honesty revealed to Jesus she was open to a new way of life.

Jesus knew the truth (v. 22), and she desired what he had. She said, "When [the Messiah] comes, he will explain everything to us" (v. 26), her quest for the truth broke down the barrier to her breakthrough.

Truth will set you free from anything that hinders and debilitates you regardless of how long it has held sway over your life.

Conclusion

The racism that divided the woman from her Lord was based on painful lies; however, the truth of who Jesus truly is tore down the wall of racism. The chance encounter was transformative. When the episode in her life was over, she had been changed into a minister. She laid down her water jar (4:28), and according to her faith, she picked up a new way of life. She became the anointed tool God used to save a town (John 4:39).

Faith & Action
Lesson Six

1) What did you learn about your faith from this chapter? (Be specific)

_____

_____

_____

_____

_____

2) In what area(s) of your life can you apply what you learned?

_____

_____

_____

_____

3) "Prayer changes things." Pray first, then take action in an area(s) of your life according to your faith.

Action Area 1:

Action Area 2:

Faith Journal

Testimony Journal

_____

_____

_____

_____

_____

_____

_____

_____

_____

_____

_____

_____

_____

_____

_____

_____

_____

_____

_____

_____

Don't Give Up on God

7

DON'T GIVE UP ON GOD

Many have undertaken to draw up an account of the things that have been fulfilled among us, ²just as they were handed down to us by those who from the first were eyewitnesses and servants of the word. ³Therefore, since I myself have carefully investigated everything from the beginning, it seemed good also to me to write an orderly account for you, most excellent Theophilus, ⁴so that you may know the certainty of the things you have been taught.

—Luke 1:1–4

¹¹Then an angel of the Lord appeared to him, standing at the right side of the altar of incense. ¹²When Zechariah saw him, he was startled and was gripped with fear. ¹³But the angel said to him: "Do not be afraid, Zechariah; your prayer has been heard. Your wife Elizabeth will bear you a son, and you are to give him the name John."

—Luke 1:11–13

Introduction

It is a privilege to have a relationship with Jesus Christ. It is an added honor to be called to write one of the Gospels. But there is an even greater distinction: God tasked Luke with investigating the validity of what Jesus did.

Some people wrote about Jesus and all that he did from eyewitness accounts (e.g., Matthew and John). Others wrote about Jesus after his death and resurrection, i.e. Paul in the Epistles. Luke, by contrast, wrote his gospel after "carefully [investigating] everything" that was ever spoken and written about Jesus. That's truly amazing.

Imagine speaking to the paralytic who was lowered through Peter's roof to be healed by Jesus (Luke 5). Imagine interviewing the woman with the issue of blood who was loosed from her infirmities (Mark 5). Imagine sitting down with the man once known as the Gadarenes demoniac (i.e., Legion) and listening to him preach the gospel (Mark 5). Can you picture the evangelist who was set free at the well (John 4) and the story she could tell you about the Lord?

Most can only dream what it was like to hear them tell about the earthly Jesus. Luke spoke with them all, and he then wrote down their testimonies.

Discussion

Luke's purpose and main point of his Gospel was to help the faith of a man by the name of Theophilus

(Luke 1:4) because the recipient had become uncertain about his faith. Luke was therefore trying to encourage his close associate.

Note Theophilus was also a patron (meaning he was wealthy and influential, e.g., as the term "most excellent" suggests) of Luke's ministry; put plainly, he financed the apostle while he was writing and researching the Gospel and the Book of Acts. He supported the work that went into producing the account, but he was struggling with his faith in the process. Somewhere along the way, Theophilus' faith had gotten weak.

As a result, Luke was writing to restore his friend's faith. The "beloved physician" (Colossians 4:14) could have started with any account in the Bible, but he chose to start with the story of John the Baptist's parents because it spoke to people struggling with their faith in the same way Theophilus was struggling with his.

In the Synoptic Gospels, Mark and Matthew wrote about John the Baptist, but Luke decided to write about the unique set of circumstances that birthed the Baptist.

John the Baptist's parents were both from the priestly line of Aaron, which meant their understanding growing up was that they were responsible for taking care of the temple. When all the other tribes inherited parcels in the Promised Land, the priestly line inherited the stewardship of God. God was their inheritance, which meant the land wouldn't take care of them—God would.

We know three things about John the Baptist's parents: 1) Zechariah and his wife, Elizabeth, were extremely old when Zechariah was called to serve as the priest before God; 2) they didn't have any children, which would have been a disgrace, but more than a disgrace, it would have said they didn't have the favor of God on their lives; 3) despite being disgraced and deprived of the personal happiness of having children, Luke found out from his investigation that they served the Lord blamelessly—i.e., they did right before God down to the letter even when they must have thought that God had not been particularly good to them.

But despite all of that—being old, being barren, and living under the stigma of divine disfavor, Zechariah was still praying and asking God to bless his wife. He was faithful in the face of uncertainty.

And on the day he went to the temple to serve, which was a long shot because selection was based on the casting of lots, when he got inside the temple, an angel met him at the altar and told him, "Zechariah, your prayer has been heard . . . Elizabeth will bear you a son, and you are to give him the name John […]" (v. 13).

Conclusion

There is only one conclusion Theophilus, which means "one who loves God," could take away from this episode in his life—and for that matter the only conclusion any of us who have put our trust in God and say we love the Lord can take away: Despite being uncertain and living with heartbreak, **don't give up on God**.

God may not always come right when you want Him, but when He does come, He's always right on time.

The Lord showed up when Zechariah least expected it. The angel met him at the altar with an answer to his prayer.

So, stay faithful. Stay true. Be blameless, for God is a rewarder of people who diligently (i.e., give steady and earnest effort) look to Him in faith and trust.

Faith & Action
Lesson Seven

1) *What did you learn about your faith from this chapter? (Be specific)*

_____

_____

_____

_____

_____

2) *In what area(s) of your life can you apply what you learned?*

_____

_____

_____

_____

_____

3) *"Prayer changes things." Pray first, then take action in an area(s) of your life according to your faith.*

Action Area 1:

Action Area 2:

Faith Journal

_____

_____

_____

_____

_____

_____

_____

_____

_____

_____

_____

_____

_____

_____

_____

_____

_____

_____

FAITH CAN MOVE MOUNTAINS
Testimony Journal

Can You Spare Some Crumbs?

8

CAN YOU SPARE SOME CRUMBS?

21Leaving that place, Jesus withdrew to the region of Tyre and Sidon.
22A Canaanite woman from that vicinity came to him, crying out,
"Lord, Son of David, have mercy on me! My daughter is suffering
terribly from demon-possession."
23Jesus did not answer a word. So his disciples came to him and
urged him, "Send her away, for she keeps crying out after us."
24He answered, "I was sent only to the lost sheep of Israel."
25The woman came and knelt before him. "Lord, help me!" she said.
26He replied, "It is not right to take the children's bread and toss it to
their dogs."
27"Yes, Lord," she said, "but even the dogs eat the crumbs that fall
from their masters' table."
28Then Jesus answered, "Woman, you have great faith! Your request
is granted." And her daughter was healed from that very hour.
—Matthew 15:21–28

Introduction

This particular scripture lesson points to the fact
that faith can sometimes come down to two approaches:

1) There's the theory of faith, and 2) there's the practice of faith.

Theory is what you believe. Theory helps you explain and understand what's going on around you in the world, and it then becomes the basis for the action(s) you take.

Practice is what you actually do in real life. For instance, Mike Tyson,[2] the infamous heavyweight boxing champion, once insisted, "Everyone has a plan until they [sic] get punched in the face." The point he was making is that anyone can have a theoretical approach to any particular situation, but the theory is only as good as the action taken in the ring of real life.

In a perfect world, what you do should be based on what you believe; however, problems occur when you don't do what you say you believe.

Faith is the same way. There is the theory of faith, and there is the practice of faith.

The story of the Canaanite woman is an illustration of how faith in practice is often contrasted with faith in theory.

But it's not the woman's faith that is the focus; it's the disciples' faith.

---

[2] Mike Tyson reigned as the undisputed heavyweight champion of the world from 1987 to 1990.

Discussion

Jesus had just entered the region of Tyre and Sidon, and as soon as he got there a woman started crying out to him, "Lord, Son of David, have mercy on me! My daughter is suffering terribly from demon-possession," but (initially) Jesus did not answer her request. He didn't say a word.

Then the story says, "So his disciples came to him and urged him, 'Send her away, for she keeps crying after us.'" Actually, she cried after Jesus, but they assumed because she wanted Jesus and they were with him, then that meant she wanted them, too.

This was their moment to put their faith into practice. Faith in theory is one thing; faith in practice is something else. They said send her away, illustrating to the Lord that their actions did not yet match their spoken belief.

Interestingly, they had just come out of what amounted to a workshop on faith (Matthew 15:1–20). They had been criticized for not washing their hands before they ate, but Jesus mercifully came to their defense.

The Lord told the Pharisees who were criticizing his disciples, well you say they break the traditions of the elders by not washing their hands before they eat, but you break the command of God (Matthew 15:1–2).

Jesus explained to the "Pharisees and teachers of the law" that they were not honoring their fathers and mothers, and their excuse was what they would use to help their parents, they had already devoted to God (cf., Corban, Mark 7:11), so they couldn't use it to help their parents.

The people were using their faith as an excuse to not help people they selfishly didn't want to help in the first place.

With that said, Jesus would have never pointed out their sin had they not called the disciples' sin out. When they criticized the disciples, Jesus showed them what they were doing wrong.

To make his point, the carpenter's son said, "What goes into a man's mouth does not make him 'unclean,' but what comes out of his mouth" (Matthew 15:10). Put another way, what they said actually showed Jesus who they really were.

In the same manner, when the Lord's disciples said send the Canaanite woman away, they were showing their true faith. They had just come out of a faith workshop, but they only understood faith in theory.

All the woman wanted was some crumbs. All she asked was, "Lord . . . have mercy on me!" (v. 22).

They were sitting at the Master's table, and He was feeding them and healing them, but they couldn't spare any crumbs of compassion for someone else in need.

Don't have the kind of faith that always look for God to feed and bless you with bread, but you can't ever spare any crumbs for somebody else.

Jesus told the woman, "I was sent only to the lost sheep of Israel."

Then the woman came and knelt down before him, "Lord, help me!" (v. 25).

Jesus said, "It is not right to take the children's bread and toss it to their dogs."

The woman said, "But even the dogs eat the crumbs that fall from their masters' table."

Conclusion

God doesn't expect you to **not** do what is right in order to be kind to someone in need, but while you're doing what you know the Lord wants you to do, can you along the way spare some crumbs for somebody else?

There is faith in theory, but **put** what you believe into practice. When God has blessed you, can you spare some crumbs for someone else who is not yet blessed?

Why? The Lord will always give you bread if you can spare some crumbs for someone else in need. That is called faith in practice.

Jesus told the woman, "Your request is granted." Despite the inconvenience, he spared her some crumbs of his mercy and grace, and her daughter was healed that very hour (v.28).

Faith & Action
Lesson Eight

1) What did you learn about your faith from this chapter? (Be specific)

_____

_____

_____

_____

2) In what area(s) of your life can you apply what you learned?

_____

_____

_____

_____

3) "Prayer changes things." Pray first, then take action in an area(s) of your life according to your faith.

Action Area 1:

Action Area 2:

Faith Journal

_____

_____

_____

_____

_____

_____

_____

_____

_____

_____

_____

_____

_____

_____

_____

_____

_____

_____

FAITH CAN MOVE MOUNTAINS
Testimony Journal

Epilogue

With rock-solid faith in the Lord, you will get the victory in life. A favorite scripture of the great generals of the faith assures, "They overcame him [i.e., Satan] by the blood of the Lamb [i.e., Jesus] and by the word of their testimony" (Revelation 12:11). "They," meaning the faithful children of God, knew that their faith is what would give them a testimony as to what the Lord can do for everyone who trusts and believes in him despite what things may look like, and he did not let them down.

When you walk in faith, you will experience victory in life. Trust and believe, for he will not disappoint you.

Further Study on Faith

Achtemeier, Paul J., Joel B. Green, and Marianne Meye Thompson. *Introducing The New Testament: Its Literature and Theology*. William B. Eerdmans Publishing Company, Grand Rapids, Michigan/Cambridge, U.K. 2001.

Brueggemann, Walter. *Interpretation: A Bible Commentary for Teaching and Preaching. Genesis*. John Knox Press, Louisville 1982.

Hare, Douglas E. *Interpretation: A Bible Commentary for Teaching and Preaching. Matthew*. John Knox Press, Louisville 1993.

Smith, Jr., D. Moody. *Abingdon New Testament Commentaries. John*. Abingdon Press, Nashville 1999.

Spivey, Robert A. and D. Moody Smith. *Anatomy Of The New Testament: A Guide to Its Structure and Meaning*. 5th Edition. Prentice Hall, Upper Saddle River, New Jersey, 1995.

Turner, Jr., William C. *From Scribble to Script: Preparing to Preach*. Morris Publishing, Kearney, NE 2003.

Willimon, William H. *Interpretation: A Bible Commentary for Teaching and Preaching. Acts*. John Knox Press, Louisville 1988.

Life Notes

Life Notes

Life Notes

About the Author

Dr. Derrick Justice is the recipient of the prestigious Jameson Jones Preaching Award from the Divinity School at Duke University. As both an English professor and a senior pastor, Dr. Justice has mastered a rare communication style that grips and transforms lives in the classroom as well as from the pulpit. Equally dynamic in speech and in print, his words and insights will literally excite as they also inspire.

www.ingramcontent.com/pod-product-compliance
Lightning Source LLC
Chambersburg PA
CBHW031628040426
42452CB00007B/724